Winds OF *praise*

12 Worship Arrangements for
One or More Wind Players
Arranged by Stan Pethel

PUBLICATIONS AVAILABLE:

SB1040 Piano / Score

SB1041 Flute / Oboe / Violin (with CD)

SB1042 Trumpet / Clarinet (with CD)

SB1043 French Horn (with CD)

SB1044 Trombone / Tuba / Cello (with CD)

SB1047 Alto Saxophone (with CD)

Shawnee Press

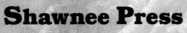

EXCLUSIVELY DISTRIBUTED BY

HAL•LEONARD®
CORPORATION

7777 W. BLUEMOUND RD. P.O. BOX 13819 MILWAUKEE, WI 53213

Visit Shawnee Press Online at **www.shawneepress.com/songbooks**

PREFACE

Winds of Praise was designed to allow for maximum flexibility of use. The uses range from full ensemble to solo instrument and piano. All of the arrangements will also work without piano. Just start at the first double bar or the pickups to the first double bar.

Here are some options:

1. Solo instrument and piano or track. The piano/score book works as accompaniment for all instruments as does the accompaniment CD.

2. Multiple instruments and piano or track. Just have one instrument play the solo part and the other(s) the ensemble part along with the piano or accompaniment CD. Use more players on the solo part if needed to project the melody.

3. For instruments only, with no piano or CD accompaniment, these combinations will work:

   a. Brass Quartet – trumpet 1 & 2 with trombone 1 & 2 parts will stand alone. Start at the first double bar.

   b. Brass Quintet or Brass Sextet – For quintet use trumpet 1 & 2, horn, trombone 1, and tuba. For sextet add trombone 2. Start at the double bar.

   c. Other ensemble combinations. As long as trumpet 1 & 2 and trombone 1 & 2 are covered, the other parts will only add to the fullness of the ensemble. Piano adds even more and fills out the harmony. For instruments only start at the double bar, with piano starting at the beginning.

   d. Remember these instrumental substitutions. Violins and oboes can play or double the flute part. Clarinets can play or double the trumpet parts. Cellos, bassoons, and baritones can play the trombone part. Bass trombone players may want to try the tuba part as well. The tuba part can also be covered by a bass setting from an electric keyboard to add depth to the sound.

These arrangements are good lengths for preludes, offertories, and featured instrumental performance in both church services and church or school concerts. The level of difficulty ranges from 2 ½ to 3. Most are also in good vocal range should you choose to add choral or congregational singing at appropriate places. If you have a rhythm section of piano, guitar, bass, and drums, there are chord symbols provided with some basic drum suggestions in the piano score.

Best wishes with these arrangements in your area of musical ministry. Let us know at Shawnee Press if you find them useful, and what else we can do to assist with your instrumental needs.

Stan Pethel

CONTENTS

Come, Now Is the Time to Worship

Flute
(Oboe, Violin)
Ensemble

Music by **BRIAN DOERKSEN**
Arranged by **STAN PETHEL**

Come, Now Is the Time to Worship

Flute
(Oboe 8vb, Violin 8vb)
Solo

Music by **BRIAN DOERKSEN**
Arranged by **STAN PETHEL**

Flute
(Violin 8vb, Oboe 8vb)
Solo

Here I Am to Worship

Music by **TIM HUGHES**
Arranged by **STAN PETHEL**

Here I Am to Worship

Flute
(Oboe, Violin)
Ensemble

Music by **TIM HUGHES**
Arranged by **STAN PETHEL**

He Is Exalted

Flute
(Oboe, Violin)
Ensemble

Music by **TWILA PARIS**
Arranged by **STAN PETHEL**

He Is Exalted

Flute
(Oboe 8vb, Violin 8vb)
Solo

Music by **TWILA PARIS**
Arranged by **STAN PETHEL**

With motion (♩. = *ca. 72*)

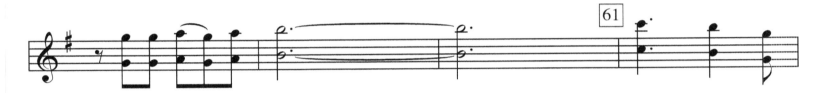

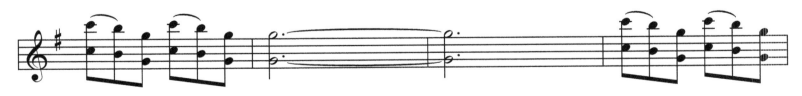

In Christ Alone

Music by **KEITH GETTY** and **STUART TOWNEND**
Arranged by **STAN PETHEL**

Flute
(Oboe, Violin)
Ensemble

In Christ Alone

Flute
(Violin, Oboe)
Solo

Music by **KEITH GETTY** *and* **STUART TOWNEND**
Arranged by **STAN PETHEL**

Flute
(Oboe, Violin)
Ensemble

Sanctuary

Music by **JOHN W. THOMPSON**
and **RANDY SCRUGGS**
Arranged by **STAN PETHEL**

Samba feel (♩ = *ca.* 112)

Sanctuary

Flute
(Violin 8vb, Oboe 8vb)
Solo

Music by **JOHN W. THOMPSON**
and **RANDY SCRUGGS**
Arranged by **STAN PETHEL**

Flute
(Violin 8vb, Oboe 8vb)
Solo

How Great Is Our God

Music by **Chris Tomlin, Jesse Reeves,** *and* **Ed Cash**
Arranged by **STAN PETHEL**

How Great Is Our God

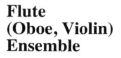

Flute
(Oboe, Violin)
Ensemble

Music by **Chris Tomlin, Jesse Reeves,**
and **Ed Cash**
Arranged by **STAN PETHEL**

As the Deer

**Flute (Oboe, Violin)
Ensemble**

Music by **MARTIN NYSTROM**
Arranged by **STAN PETHEL**

Flute
(Violin 8vb, Oboe 8vb)
Solo

As the Deer

Music by **MARTIN NYSTROM**
Arranged by **STAN PETHEL**

Lord, I Lift Your Name on High

Flute
(Oboe, Violin)
Ensemble

Music by **RICK POUNDS**
Arranged by **STAN PETHEL**

Lord, I Lift Your Name on High

Flute
(Violin 8vb, Oboe 8vb)
Solo

Music by **RICK POUNDS**
Arranged by *STAN PETHEL*

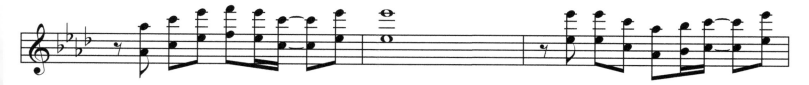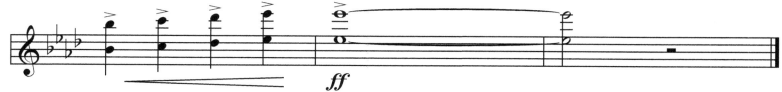

Above All

Flute
(Oboe, Violin)
Ensemble

Music by **LENNY LEBRANC** *and* **PAUL BALOCHE**
Arranged by **STAN PETHEL**

Flute
(Violin 8vb, Oboe 8vb)
Solo

Above All

Music by **LENNY LEBRANC** and **PAUL BALOCHE**
Arranged by **STAN PETHEL**

29

Jesus, Draw Me Close

Flute (Oboe, Violin)
Ensemble

Music by **RICK FOUNDS**
Arranged by **STAN PETHEL**

Flute
(Violin 8vb, Oboe 8vb)
Solo

Jesus, Draw Me Close

Music by **RICK FOUNDS**
Arranged by **STAN PETHEL**

Shine, Jesus, Shine

Flute
(Oboe, Violin)
Ensemble

Music by **GRAHAM KENDRICK**
Arranged by **STAN PETHEL**

Shine, Jesus, Shine

Flute
(Violin 8vb, Oboe 8vb)
Solo

Music by **GRAHAM KENDRICK**
Arranged by **STAN PETHEL**

You Are My All In All

Flute (Oboe, Violin)
Ensemble

Music by **DENNIS JERNIGAN**
Arranged by **STAN PETHEL**

You Are My All In All

Flute
(Violin 8vb, Oboe 8vb)
Solo

Music by **DENNIS JERNIGAN**
Arranged by **STAN PETHEL**

PIANO & ORGAN COLLECTIONS
from Shawnee Press

BEGINNING ORGANIST – VOLUME 1
by Darwin Wolford
Each piece is carefully edited, complete with fingerings and pedal indications, making it an excellent teaching resource. Includes: "Duet" by Handel, "From Heaven on High" by Reger, "Voluntary" by Boellmann, "Andante" by Zollner, and "In Dulci Jubilo" by Bach.
_____ 35001866 Organ Solo $14.99

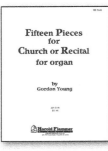

FIFTEEN PIECES FOR CHURCH OR RECITAL
by Gordon Young
Includes: Air • Antiphon • Bachiana • Benedictus • Canzona • Concertino • Divertissement • Glorificamus • Marche • Offertorium • Postludium • Prelude on "Blessed Assurance" • Toccata • Trumpet Gigue • Trumpet Voluntary.
_____ 35006677 Organ Solo $19.99

GO OUT IN JOY – FESTIVE POSTLUDES FOR PIANO
A variety of styles and difficulty levels are included, with careful attention paid to choose hymns that have the spirit of celebration in both tune and text. Enjoy the work of Vicki Tucker Courtney, Cindy Berry, Brad Nix, Alex-Zsolt, Hojun Lee and others!
_____ 35028092 Piano Solo $16.99

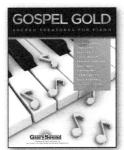

GOSPEL GOLD
Featuring Arrangements from: Cindy Berry, Patti Drennan, Mark Hayes, Lloyd Larson, and others
Some of today's best pianists and arrangers have gathered to celebrate the best timeless gospel hymns in a new compilation sure to be a hit with any church pianist. 17 songs, including: Stand Up, Stand Up for Jesus • 'Tis So Sweet to Trust in Jesus • Just a Closer Walk with Thee • Do Lord • Rock of Ages • He Keeps Me Singing • and many more.
_____ 35027306 Piano Solo $16.99

GOSPEL GOLD – VOLUME 2
Stretch your offertory options with this brilliant collection from some of today's most respected piano arrangers: Mary McDonald, Pamela Robertson, Shirley Brendlinger, Brad Nix, James Koerts, Carolyn Hamlin and others.
_____ 35028093 Piano Solo $16.99

HYMNS OF GRATEFUL PRAISE
arr. Lee Dengler
Includes: For the Beauty of the Earth • Joyful, Joyful We Adore Thee • Morning Has Broken • Fairest Lord Jesus • Now Thank We All Our God • Holy God We Praise Thy Name • All Creatures of Our God and King • Praise to the Lord the Almighty • Praise Him! Praise Him! • and more.
_____ 35028339 Piano Solo $16.99

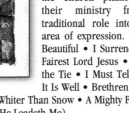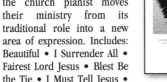

IMAGES
arr. Heather Sorenson
When combined with the innovative visual supplement, the church pianist moves their ministry from its traditional role into a new area of expression. Includes: Beautiful • I Surrender All • Fairest Lord Jesus • Blest Be the Tie • I Must Tell Jesus • It Is Well • Brethren We Have Met to Worship • Whiter Than Snow • A Mighty Fortress • The Journey (with He Leadeth Me).
_____ 35028265 Piano Solo $16.99
_____ 35028266 Listening CD $16.99
_____ 35028277 Piano Solos Book/
                  DVD-ROM Pack $29.99

JOY TO THE WORLD
arr. Jack Jones
Includes: Joy to the World • Angels We Have Heard on High • Coventry Carol • Deck the Hall • Ding Dong! Merrily on High! • Good Christians, All Rejoice • Good People All This Christmas Time • Infant Holy, Infant Lowly • Rise Up, Shepherd, and Follow.
_____ 35028373 Organ Solo $16.99

MUSIC OF THE MASTERS FOR THE MASTER
Using a classical theme or genre as the basis for each piece, the composer weds a time-honored hymn to bring these beloved themes into the sanctuary. Included in this thoughtful assembly is the writing of Mary McDonald, Cindy Berry, Carolyn Hamlin, Joseph Martin, Alex-Zsolt, Jack Jones, James Michael Stevens and many others.
_____ 35028091 Piano Solo $19.99

SIMPLY BEAUTIFUL
Includes: What a Friend We Have in Jesus • Be Thou My Vision • Tis So Sweet to Trust In Jesus • I Am Bound for the Promised Land • Shades of Dawn • Softly and Tenderly • I Am His and He Is Mine • Jesus Keep Me Near the Cross • Shall We Gather At the River • and many more.
_____ 35027735 Piano Solo $16.95

SNOW FALLING ON IVORY
From tender carols of reflections to sparkling songs of joy, this collection has something for everybody. Includes: Dance at the Manger • Ding Dong Merrily on High • Gesu Bambino • Go, Tell It on the Mountain • In the Bleak Mid-Winter • It Came Upon a Midnight Clear • Let All Mortal Flesh Keep Silence • and more.
_____ 35020710 Piano Solo $24.95

SNOW FALLING ON IVORY – VOLUME 2
Pianists may play the arrangements as piano solos or perform them in tandem with the optional instrumental descants for something truly special. Arrangers include: Joseph Martin, John Purifoy, Lee Dengler, Vicki Tucker Courtney, Brad Nix, Harry Strack, Matt Hyzer, Shirley Brendlinger, Alex-Zsolt, James Koerts and Joel Raney.
_____ 35028386 Piano Solo $19.99

Shawnee Press
EXCLUSIVELY DISTRIBUTED BY

HAL•LEONARD® CORPORATION
7777 W. BLUEMOUND RD. P.O. BOX 13819 MILWAUKEE, WI 53213

Prices, contents, and availability subject to change without notice.